100 Best Quotes About Improving Yourself

Jesse Worth

100 Best Quotes About Improving Yourself

Copyright © 2023 Jesse Worth

All rights reserved.

ISBN: 9798851269639
Imprint: Independently published

DEDICATION

This book is dedicated to all those who have embarked on the beautiful journey of self-improvement.

It is for those who strive to grow, evolve, and become the best version of themselves.

With sincere admiration,

                      Jesse Worth

100 Best Quotes About Improving Yourself

Your Review Matters

Your review could really help us get the word out about this book. Please take the time to leave a review. Use the QR Code below to access the Amazon review form.

Thank you for your support!

100 Best Quotes About Improving Yourself

CONTENTS

Quote #1   9

Closing Thoughts   59

100 Best Quotes About Improving Yourself

QUOTE #1

"If you want to live a happy life, tie it to a goal, not to people or things."

-Albert Einstein

QUOTE #2

"We must accept finite disappointment, but never lose infinite hope."

-Martin Luther King, Jr.

QUOTE #3

"Discipline is choosing between what you want now and what you want most."

-Augusta F. Kantra

QUOTE #4

"Don't let what you cannot do interfere with what you can do."

-John Wooden

QUOTE #5

"Success is walking from failure to failure with no loss of enthusiasm."

-Winston Churchill

QUOTE #6

"The greater danger for most of us lies not in setting our aim too high and falling short, but in setting our aim too low and achieving our mark."

-Michelangelo

QUOTE #7

"Commit to lifelong learning. Stay curious, stay humble, and keep seeking knowledge and wisdom."

-Oprah Winfrey

QUOTE #8

"Self-control is the chief element in self-respect, and self-respect is the chief element in courage."

-Thucydides

QUOTE #9

"When it is obvious that the goals cannot be reached, don't adjust your goals, adjust the action steps."

-Confucius

QUOTE #10

"Innovation distinguishes between a leader and a follower."

-Steve Jobs

QUOTE #11

"Every morning, we get a chance to be different. A chance to change. A chance to be better."

-Alan Bonner

QUOTE #12

"The most difficult thing in life is to know yourself."

-Thales

QUOTE #13

"Discipline is the bridge between goals and accomplishment."

-Jim Rohn

QUOTE #14

"There is little success where there is little laughter."

-Andrew Carnegie

QUOTE #15

"Embrace a growth mindset and constantly challenge yourself to learn and improve."

-Satya Nadella

QUOTE #16

"Your most unhappy customers are your greatest source of learning."

-Bill Gates

QUOTE #17

"The curious paradox is that when I accept myself just as I am, then I can change."

-Carl Rogers

QUOTE #18

"There is no substitute for victory."

-Douglas MacArthur

QUOTE #19

"Set your goals high, and don't stop till you get there."

-Bo Jackson

QUOTE #20

"Champions keep playing until they get it right."

-Billie Jean King

QUOTE #21

"Much effort, much prosperity."

-Euripides

QUOTE #22

"The biggest adventure you can take is to live the life of your dreams."

-Oprah Winfrey

QUOTE #23

"In coaching, continuous learning is not only an option, but a necessity. The moment you think you know it all, you've already fallen behind."

-Bill Belichick

QUOTE #24

"If one does not know to which port one is sailing, no wind is favorable."

-Seneca

QUOTE #25

"Success is the result of perfection, hard work, learning from failure, loyalty, and persistence."

-Colin Powell

QUOTE #26

"When we seek to discover the best in others, we somehow bring out the best in ourselves."

-William Arthur Ward

QUOTE #27

"Discipline is choosing between what you want now and what you want most."

-Abraham Lincoln

QUOTE #28

"Doubt kills more dreams than failure ever will."

-Suzy Kassem

QUOTE #29

"You can't let life happen to you; you have to make life happen."

-Idowu Koyenikan

QUOTE #30

"Fear is a reaction. Courage is a decision."

-Winston Churchill

QUOTE #31

"Happiness and freedom begin with a clear understanding of one principle: Some things are within our control, and some things are not."

-Epictetus

QUOTE #32

"Set a goal to take on new challenges and responsibilities that push you outside of your comfort zone and encourage growth."

-Sheryl Sandberg

QUOTE #33

"Confront the dark parts of yourself, and work to banish them with illumination and forgiveness. Your willingness to wrestle with your demons will cause your angels to sing."

-August Wilson

QUOTE #34

"Failure is not an option."

-Gene Kranz

QUOTE #35

"The only person you are destined to become is the person you decide to be."

-Ralph Waldo Emerson

QUOTE #36

"You are braver than you believe, stronger than you seem and smarter than you think."

-A.A. Milne

QUOTE #37

"The road to success is dotted with many tempting parking spaces."

-Will Rogers

QUOTE #38

"Success is not the key to happiness. Happiness is the key to success. If you love what you are doing, you will be successful."

-Albert Schweitzer

QUOTE #39

"Make continuous learning a habit by attending workshops, conferences, and industry events to stay updated with the latest trends and innovations."

-Tim Cook

QUOTE #40

"Success is best when it's shared."

-Howard Schultz

QUOTE #41

"You have been criticizing yourself for years, and it hasn't worked. Try approving of yourself and see what happens."

-Louise L. Hay

QUOTE #42

"The only journey is the one within."

-Rainer Maria Rilke

QUOTE #43

"Make it a goal to learn something new every day, no matter how small."

-Richard Branson

QUOTE #44

"It's not whether you get knocked down; it's whether you get up."

-Vince Lombardi

QUOTE #45

"You can't let praise or criticism get to you. It's a weakness to get caught up in either one."

-John Wooden

QUOTE #46

"The ability to discipline yourself to delay gratification in the short term in order to enjoy greater rewards in the long term is the indispensable prerequisite for success."

-Brian Tracy

QUOTE #47

"Insecurity is a waste of time."

-Diane von Furstenberg

QUOTE #48

"You can have anything you want if you are willing to give up the belief that you can't have it."

-Abraham Lincoln

QUOTE #49

"Knowing yourself is the beginning of all wisdom."

-Aristotle

QUOTE #50

"Set goals that make you stretch. Aim for the exceptional."

-Jim Rohn

QUOTE #51

"If opportunity doesn't knock, build a door."

-Milton Berle

QUOTE #52

"Courage is what it takes to stand up and speak; courage is also what it takes to sit down and listen."

-Winston Churchill

QUOTE #53

"No person has the power to have everything they want, but it is in their power not to want what they don't have, and to cheerfully put to good use what they do have."

-Seneca

QUOTE #54

"You must be the change you wish to see in the world."

-Gregg Popovich

QUOTE #55

"Your work is going to fill a large part of your life, and the only way to be truly satisfied is to do what you believe is great work."

-Steve Jobs

QUOTE #56

"The trouble with not having a goal is that you can spend your life running up and down the field and never score."

-Bill Copeland

QUOTE #57

"Make continuous learning a priority by dedicating a specific amount of time each week to acquire new skills or deepen existing ones."

-Jack Ma

QUOTE #58

"You are never really playing an opponent. You are playing yourself, your own highest standards and when you reach your limits, that is real joy."

-Dan Daly

QUOTE #59

"Success is the progressive realization of a worthy goal or ideal."

-Earl Nightingale

QUOTE #60

"The wise man does not lay up his own treasures. The more he gives to others, the more he has for his own."

-Lao Tzu

QUOTE #61

"I couldn't wait for success, so I went ahead without it."

-Jonathan Winters

QUOTE #62

"You have to expect things of yourself before you can do them."

-Serena Williams

QUOTE #63

"He who fears death will never do anything worthy of a man who is alive."

-Seneca

QUOTE #64

"Discipline is the soul of an army. It makes small numbers formidable; procures success to the weak, and esteem to all."

-George Washington

QUOTE #65

"The first rule is to keep an untroubled spirit. The second is to look things in the face and know them for what they are."

-Marcus Aurelius

QUOTE #66

"The moment you give up all thought of retreat or surrender, you become an unstoppable force."

-Tommy Newberry

QUOTE #67

"Comparison is the thief of joy."

-Theodore Roosevelt

QUOTE #68

"Set a goal to share your knowledge and expertise with others through teaching, mentoring, or writing to reinforce your own understanding and contribute to the growth of others.

-Malala Yousafzai

QUOTE #69

"Love yourself; you won't regret it ever."

-M.F. Moonzajer

QUOTE #70

"Change is the essence of life; be willing to surrender what you are for what you could become."

-Reinhold Niebuhr

QUOTE #71

"The only way to prove that you're a good sport is to lose."

-Ernie Banks

QUOTE #72

"Create a goal to build a strong network of professionals in your industry to foster collaboration and learning from others."

-Mary Barra

QUOTE #73

"The difference between ordinary and extraordinary is that little extra."

-Jimmy Johnson

QUOTE #74

"The best way to appreciate your job is to imagine yourself without one."

-Oscar Wilde

QUOTE #75

"I walk slowly, but I never walk backward."

-Abraham Lincoln

QUOTE #76

"The whole future lies in uncertainty; live immediately."

-Seneca

QUOTE #77

"With self-discipline, most anything is possible."

-Theodore Roosevelt

QUOTE #78

"Continuous improvement is better than delayed perfection."

-Mark Twain

QUOTE #79

"The tragedy in life doesn't lie in not reaching your goal. The tragedy lies in having no goal to reach."

-Benjamin Mays

QUOTE #80

"Success is not a destination, it's a journey."

-Zig Ziglar

QUOTE #81

"The greatest leader is not necessarily the one who does the greatest things. They are the one that gets the people to do the greatest things."

-Ronald Reagan

QUOTE #82

"Impatience never commanded success."

-Edwin H. Chapin

QUOTE #83

"The Navy SEALs motto is 'The only easy day was yesterday.' The more you push yourself and the more you push your teammates, the better you become."

-William McRaven

QUOTE #84

"It's amazing what you can accomplish if you do not care who gets the credit."

-Harry S. Truman

QUOTE #85

"Goals are dreams with deadlines."

-Diana Scharf Hunt

QUOTE #86

"The first rule is to keep an untroubled spirit. The second is to look things in the face and know them for what they are."

-Marcus Aurelius

QUOTE #87

"By improving yourself, the world is made better. Be not afraid of growing too slowly. Be afraid only of standing still."

-Benjamin Franklin

QUOTE #88

"Success is finding satisfaction in giving a little more than you take."

-Christopher Reeve

QUOTE #89

"When you set goals, something inside of you starts saying, 'Let's go, let's go,' and ceilings start to move up."

-Zig Ziglar

QUOTE #90

"Success is a lousy teacher. It seduces smart people into thinking they can't lose."

-Bill Gates

QUOTE #91

"The soul becomes dyed with the color of its thoughts."

-Marcus Aurelius

QUOTE #92

"Set a goal to read a certain number of books or articles each month to expand your knowledge and perspective."

-Indra Nooyi

QUOTE #93

"Our deepest fear is not that we are inadequate. Our deepest fear is that we are powerful beyond measure."

-Marianne Williamson

QUOTE #94

"The mind is everything. What you think, you become."

-Buddha

QUOTE #95

"In the middle of difficulty lies opportunity."

-Albert Einstein

QUOTE #96

"Invest in your personal development by seeking mentors or coaches who can guide and inspire you on your journey."

-Jeff Bezos

QUOTE #97

"You need a plan to build a house. To build a life, it is even more important to have a plan or goal."

-Zig Ziglar

QUOTE #98

"When you come to the end of your rope, tie a knot and hang on."

-Franklin D. Roosevelt

QUOTE #99

"Hard work beats talent when talent doesn't work hard."

-Tim Notke

QUOTE #100

"Invest in yourself. You can afford it. Trust me."

-Warren Buffett

CLOSING THOUGHTS

As you navigate the ups and downs of your self-improvement journey, remember that progress is not always linear. There may be setbacks, challenges, and moments of doubt, but stay resilient and keep moving forward.

Let these quotes be your companions, your motivators, and your reminders that you have the power to shape your destiny. May they serve as constant reminders that you are capable of remarkable growth and transformation.

Embrace the wisdom within these pages, let it guide you in your pursuit of self-improvement, and may it empower you to create a life filled with purpose, fulfillment, and self-discovery.

100 Best Quotes About Improving Yourself

LOOKING FOR MORE?

AVAILABLE NOW AT AMAZON.COM

100 Best Quotes About Improving Yourself